A CENTURY OF CHRISTIAN SERVICE

LECTOR HOUSE PUBLIC DOMAIN WORKS

A CENTURY OF CHRISTIAN SERVICE

CHARLES SILVESTER HORNE

ISBN: 978-93-5420-878-2

Published: 1893

© 2021
LECTOR HOUSE LLP

LECTOR HOUSE LLP
E-MAIL: lectorpublishing@gmail.com

*"Great men have been among us; hands that penned,
And tongues that uttered wisdom."*

KENSINGTON CHAPEL

A CENTURY OF CHRISTIAN SERVICE
KENSINGTON CONGREGATIONAL CHURCH
1793–1893

BY

C. SILVESTER HORNE, M.A.
MINISTER OF KENSINGTON CHAPEL

WITH FOURTEEN ILLUSTRATIONS

MDCCCXCIII

PREFACE

In placing this volume in the hands of his congregation, as a memorial of the centenary of Kensington Chapel, the writer has one or two words to say to them. They will easily see that there is here no attempt to supersede Dr. Stoughton's excellent and well-known history of our Church, entitled "Congregationalism in the Court Suburb." For all detail of our work, as well as for most delightful reminiscences of the ministers who laboured here, they are referred to Dr. Stoughton's book. The letterpress of this little book is an introduction to the pictures it contains, and it is an attempt to trace the rise and progress of the *Church*, rather than to dwell on the interesting features of individual ministries. This has, as the writer feels, limited the interest of the book somewhat; but he relies largely on the illustrations to commend it to those who have some sympathy with the Church whose doings it briefly chronicles. He has only to add that his best thanks are due to Mr. Sidney Davie, who has given him valued assistance in the reproduction of the photographs; and to Mr. Edward Spicer for very much co-operation in bringing out this memorial volume. But especially is he indebted to the "member of the congregation," whose name he may not mention, who so kindly wrote the notice of the three and a half years of the present ministry.

Kensington, *April*, 1893.

CONTENTS

LIST OF ILLUSTRATIONS

HORNTON STREET CHAPEL

I

FORMING THE CHURCH

THERE is but little of the romance of history associated with the story of the Nonconformity of the last hundred years. The Free Churches that arose in England a century ago began with all the advantages of toleration. Their members were not objects of persecution, and the chapels that formed their local habitations had no longer to be built in obscure courts that testified to the unpopularity, and possibly the irregularity, of their existence. Churches that have such an inheritance as ours lose, no doubt, much of the stimulus which those enjoy that have great traditions of heroism and fidelity through stern seasons of suffering for conscience' sake. In the absence of such stirring pages from our history, we may well be thankful that so much remains which we may regard with especial gratitude to God, in the consistently true and honourable service rendered to the cause of Christ through four generations by the ministers and members of our Church. The story of Kensington Chapel for the hundred years of its history has been that of a succession of able and devoted ministers, supported by a Church of consecrated men and women, who have not unworthily represented the best traditions of the Nonconformity of the last century. Neither has the atmosphere of the Court suburb injuriously affected the definite and resolute Dissenting attitude of the community. The first document issued by the founders of the Church contained an explicit avowal that they were "Dissenters from the established mode of worship in this country"; and any subsequent movement of thought has only been toward a clearer apprehension of those great positive beliefs which form the permanent *raison d'être* of a Congregational Church. Mr. Faulkner, whose history of old Kensington is full of interesting information, is a good Church and State man, and quite above suspicion as to the orthodoxy of his opinions; but he bears testimony to the Independents that we are "a sect, the most respectable, and usually considered the most enlightened among Protestant Dissenters." Probably this was not committing himself to much in Mr. Faulkner's opinion: and possibly some may be found who think that our special temptation has lain in the direction of our respectability; but we must accept, with all the graciousness of which we are capable, this tribute to the fact that our founders honourably sustained the traditions of our denomination. And what is equally remarkable, they succeeded in informing even an outsider like Mr. Faulkner of their primary contention—surely no small achievement!—for he writes of us: "They are amenable as a religious society only to the jurisdiction of Christ." In other respects also he does no injustice to the Independent position.

Of the Kensington of 1793 I need not say much; for most of those who read this little book will be quite familiar with the astonishing change that has come over this locality since then. We like to recall the fields and woods through which the first seat-holders of Hornton Street Chapel walked to worship on the Sunday, even though the thought suggests melancholy reflections on our own loss in this respect. We are more content to have a century of time between ourselves and the footpads who infested the road that led to London. It appears that in 1820, when Mr. Faulkner was completing his history, a new church had been erected in Marylebone; and we are congratulated on the fact, because the joint parishes of Kensington and Paddington contain as many as twelve thousand people! And as for some years previous the great increase in the population had been causing considerable anxiety, and even alarm, we may easily estimate the paucity of the population of Kensington in 1793.

The year of our origin is famous in history as the French Revolution year. We cannot forget to what gloomy forebodings, as to the future of religion, that momentous event gave rise. It is not of course anything heroic, but it is not without its sublime side, that amid the wild and violent prophesyings of that time, the founders of this Church sat quietly down to discuss plans and estimates for erecting a meeting-house for those to worship in who, as they believed, would still desire to seek the Lord, when all the "fool-fury of the Seine" was remembered only with horror and pity. Theirs was a sound, substantial faith that was not frightened by chimeras, nor even dismayed by actual portents as alarming as the French Revolution. When a State has thrown over its Church with such violence as was used in France, it was surely something to belong to a Church that asked nothing, and expected nothing, from the State, except freedom to do its work unpatronised and unmolested.

While March, 1793, is the date of the first public document introducing the new church to the inhabitants of Kensington, it is quite clear that a quiet and effective spiritual work had been proceeding in a very simple way for some time previous to the erection of Hornton Street Chapel. This work was largely due to Mr. Saunders, the "body coachman" of George III., who was in the habit of providing His Majesty with religious tracts, and who had now retired to Kensington, where he was apparently the guiding spirit of a small conventicle "in a very humble dwelling." In such apostolic simplicity the Church began, and in course of time there was a sufficient nucleus of members and sympathisers with the freer methods of worship of the Dissenters, as to justify the issuing of the following most significant appeal, which stands as the beginning of the Church records, but has no date attached:—

> "To the friends of Religious Liberty, Sincere Christianity, and of Benevolent dispositions, etc.,—

> "We the Undersigned, of Whom, some have been educated in the principles of the Established Church of Scotland, and Others in that Class of dissenters in England, whose principles, Opinions and Faith, is the most generally Consonant To, and founded on the Word of God, as Revealed in the Scriptures of the Old and New Testament, and of These Essential Doctrines of Christianity

as Professed by both the National Churches of England and Scotland;—Being therefore dissenters from the Established Mode of Worship in this Country, and being situated at a great distance from any place of Worship Agreable to the dictates of our Consciences, We, from pure Motives of Religion and Piety Alone, for conveniancy to Ourselves and Familys, and to Others who may be like-minded with Us in Matters of Religion, Do Propose, Under the favour and Blessing of divine Providence, to Erect and Build a Temple for the Worship of Almighty God, in the Parish of Kensington, and County of Middlesex.

"We Profess Our Religious Opinions to be, According to the Rites and forms of Worship, as well as of the Doctrines, and Discipline Agreed Upon in the Confession of Faith, by the Assembly of Divines at Westminster, (So far as the Circumstances of our Situation will admit of,) we wish to follow Their Soundness of Faith, Purity and Simplicity of Worship, As far as we judge them founded on the Word of God, and Agreable to the Standard of Truth, Contained in the Holy Scriptures; The Alone Unerring Guide of Faith and Manners;

"We therefore invite the Serious Christian, The friends and lovers of Gospel Truths, to join with us in this good Undertaking, To promote the Glory of God, The interests of true Religion, and The Eternal Happiness of Ourselves and fellow Christians, Having nothing in View, but to forward the Attainment of These Great Objects, We leave the Briers, and Thorny Fields of disputation and false Philosophy, of factious politicks, and Jarring interests of Ambitious Men, 'That we may lead quiet and peacable lives in all Godliness and honesty,' as Commanded 1 Tim. ii. 1, 2."

Closely following this, apparently, was a somewhat similar appeal, dated March, 1793, which shows, however, that the "friends of religious liberty, sincere Christianity, and of benevolent dispositions" had sufficiently responded to the first appeal to justify very practical measures being taken. The second document reads as follows:—

"KENSINGTON. *March.* 1793.

"To the Friends of Christianity and Religious Liberty,—

"We the Undersigned having been educated in the Religious principles of protestant Dissenters, Do from Motives of Religion and Piety, for Conveniancy to Ourselves and families, and to Others who may be like Minded with us in Matters of Religion, being likewise Solicited by Many Serious, Welldisposed Christians, and depending on the blessing of divine Providence, With the Mild Government of this Country, have resolved to erect a Chapel for the Worship of Almighty God in the Parish of Kensington,

"For this purpose we have taken a Suitable Piece of Ground

on a long Lease, and Engaged to Erect, and Compleat a Building, Estimated at Upwards of £900, Which Work is Already began and now carrying on, We are therefore induced to Solicit the Aid and Assistance of all Liberal Minded, and Benevolent Christians, to enable us to finish and Compleat So Good an Undertaking, hoping that we shall thereby promote the Glory of God, and the Interests of true Religion and Vertue, Having Nothing in View but to forward the Attainment of these great Objects,

"All Voluntary Gifts and Contributions, from Societies or Individuals, Which are hereby humbly solicited, will be thankfully received, and gratefully acknowledged by,

JOHN BROADWOOD,
JAMES MACINTOSH,
JAMES GRAY,   }   *Trustees."*
WILLIAM FORSYTH,

Estimates even in those days were liable to be exceeded, so that we are not surprised to find that "upwards of £900" meant, in plain figures, £2000, for which sum Robert Saunderson contracted with John Broadwood and the other trustees to erect Hornton Street Chapel and buildings. It is a matter worthy of note that one whose name was destined to receive such world-wide renown, as the founder of the great firm of Broadwood & Sons, manufacturers of pianos, should have been one of the founders of this Christian Church. He is described as "a Harpsichord Maker," and was evidently of great service to the society, not only in the preliminary business arrangements, but subsequently in introducing the first organ and developing the musical service. But with the work of building well in hand, we may regard the new Church as fairly launched, and reserve our story of its opening history for the next chapter.

II

CONSOLIDATION: THE FIRST MINISTRY

It is interesting to notice that the positive principles uniting the first members of the society were as yet very indefinite. They had clearly not formulated in their own minds any very distinct doctrine of the Church. They assembled together because they had a preference for the freer form of service of Nonconformity, and wished to worship God after the manner most consonant with their own feelings. There were associated in the congregation Dissenters of many varieties of thought, and, no doubt, of differing degrees of Dissent. It was a matter of indifference to them what might be the denominational preferences of their minister. The first invitation was sent forth by the "trustees and subscribers," and was addressed to the Rev. John Lake, M.A., of whose views as to Church Government we know nothing, but have some reason to suppose he was a Presbyterian. This lack of any positive basis of Church fellowship was a somewhat serious obstacle to the spiritual progress of the community; and, indeed, the early records of the Church are a most instructive commentary on the necessity of trying to realise the Scriptural conception. The purely business aspect of their undertaking was for some years the most prominent one. The members of the society did not meet on a purely spiritual basis: and very imperfectly realised that the great mission of the Church was not accomplished by the provision of opportunities for their particular form of worship. Hence we are not surprised that some of the first ministers were often pained by the commercial spirit that at times prevailed in the deliberations of those responsible for carrying on the work.

With the same simplicity and modesty that had characterised the initiation of the work, the chapel was apparently opened with little or no ceremony, or blowing of trumpets. Not a reference do the minutes contain to any inauguration meeting. Notice was sent to "the Right Reverend Father in God, Beilby, by Divine Providence Lord Bishop of London," informing him that the Chapel had been erected as a place of worship for Dissenters, and requesting him to register it in his registry, "pursuant to the Act of Toleration." Comfortable in the possession of his lordship's nominal consent, and august episcopal sanction, the society proceeded to approach the Rev. John Neal Lake, M.A., at that time resident at Walthamstow, with a view to inducing him to undertake the ministry at Kensington. Some sixty names were attached to the invitation; and, in an admirably-worded reply, Mr. Lake accepted the position in November, 1794.

With a pastor of their choice happily settled among them, the time for entering into a closer and more spiritual bond had clearly come. The tie of a subscription to the new building was not a sufficient one for a community that was organised for the purpose of extending the kingdom of God: and hence we are fully prepared for the very simple and beautiful service held on March 8th, 1795, when "a special meeting was held at the Chapel in the afternoon of as many as were desirous of joining as members and communicants at the Lord's Table, when Mr. Lake attended and entered into religious conversation with those present, to whom he also delivered a suitable exhortation." To those who feel the supreme importance of the Church, as distinguished from either the outward building or the particular minister, this is a memorable record. This building of the living stones into a Church of Jesus Christ is far more significant than the erection of a chapel. And this warm-hearted brotherhood of Christian men and women has continued in the faith and service of Christ, in unbroken succession, for a hundred years. The first Communion service was evidently a very solemn and impressive time. Even the minutes of the Church book lose the atmosphere of formality. We learn how Mr. Lake descended from the pulpit to the Communion table, where "a linen cloth and elements" had been previously laid;[1] how the "great pew" and the adjoining pews were filled with communicants; how, after the distribution of the elements, Mr. Lake returned to the pulpit and delivered an exhortation. "Upon the whole, it was a good day to many present, and, it is to be hoped, a day to be remembered," writes the Secretary, and proceeds to record the names and addresses of the "occasional communicants" who were present.

Whether our good friend, the Secretary, exhausted himself with this description, or became less industrious than formerly, we cannot say. Possibly the unexciting but important work of the infant community seemed to him to require not even the very qualified notoriety of a minute-book. Certain it is that until May, 1798, there is but little recorded; and then "another hand" writes a short account of the monthly prayer meeting of the London Missionary Society, which, we are informed, was instituted "for the purpose of sending Christian missionaries to Otaheité, Africa, and other distant places." This prayer meeting was held "by rotation" at Kensington, and marks the beginning of the missionary interest of Kensington Chapel. Mr. Faulkner, in his notice of us, says that an auxiliary missionary society was connected with the chapel, "which, by means of contributions of one penny per week, raises the sum of nearly one hundred pounds per annum." This excellent systematic organisation of missionary interest, enlisting the rich and poor alike in the work by means of a modest and regular subscription, was a very satisfactory application of the business traditions of the Church to the problem of increasing the offerings for missionary enterprise. Possibly, after the lapse of nearly a hundred years, there are some who might find it a helpful and valuable thing to themselves and others to revive an old tradition.

---

[1] Mr. William Holborn, our Church Secretary, informs me that the cup with handles is the original communion cup. It is made of lustred pewter. When the number of communicants increased, one of the deacons remembered that he had a cup at home which was suitable for the purpose. He accordingly produced the second cup, which bears underneath it the words "a friend of the cause." The metal of which this cup is made is matter of conjecture.

THE FIRST COMMUNION CUPS

There is no account given in the minutes of Mr. Lake's resignation, but our friend Mr. Faulkner assures us, with no doubt some inward satisfaction to himself, that he at length quitted "the Dissenting interest for a curacy in the Established Church, where he sustained a respectable and useful character to the day of his death." It would be idle to pay even the tribute of a regret to this secession of ninety years ago. And it must be clear to all that one with Episcopal leanings was not the person needed to lead the people in the complete consolidation of a Congregational Church. Mr. Lake's resignation prepared the way for a sounder and healthier development of Church life and government.

PORTRAIT OF REV. JOHN CLAYTON

III

A BRIEF MINISTRY—REV. JOHN CLAYTON

It was in the month of May, 1801, that the members of the congregation united in a very earnest call to Mr. John Clayton to become their minister. As no fewer than a hundred names appear as signatories, we may infer that considerable progress had been made under Mr. Lake's ministry. Mr. Clayton was still formally unordained, though he had been assistant minister to the Rev. John Winter at Newbury for one year since leaving college. He was barely twenty-one years of age when he came to Kensington to take up the work of the pastorate. The portrait of him that adorns the Deacons' Vestry, and which is here reproduced, was clearly taken in the maturity of middle-life. He maintained admirably the traditions of the Clayton family. His father, the Rev. John Clayton, was a well-known divine, of the most approved style of pulpit manners. We read with a kind of awe of his "thickly-powdered head" and his general magnificence of demeanour. Both his sons, George and John, inherited their father's ideal. We have heard it said that the Kensington congregation has never assembled punctually on Sunday morning since John Clayton's day. It was part of the service to watch the procession of their minister from the vestry to the pulpit. Young as he was, he bore himself so bravely, in full canonicals, with gloved hands and dignified movements, that it is no wonder the congregation conceived a great admiration for his person. No one can look at his portrait without perceiving that he was a man of commanding presence; and we surely cannot wonder if he knew it, and utilised it to the best advantage. And it is only just to him to add, that the effect of his preaching was by no means due solely, or mainly, to his striking appearance. He was a man of great mental abilities, and had had considerable culture. He was thus admirably adapted in many ways to the sphere he was called to occupy. With a liking for the best society, and a distinguished appearance, his courtly habits of speech and carriage gained him a deference that was not commonly paid to Dissenting preachers. If the assiduous cultivation of these personal characteristics had tended to make him less alive to the spiritual necessities of his people, we should have been justified in depreciating them. But it had not that effect. One has only to read the energetic charge, which his father delivered to him at the ordination service at Kensington, to see that the fastidiousness of outward manner and apparel of the elder Clayton were not incompatible with a directness, incisiveness, and even vehemence of speech, that the warmest partisan might covet. It seems probable that John Clayton took his father's advice not to be an "unfaithful, accommodating pastor" in its most literal sense. He had been told in the ordination charge not only "to feed the flock, but to *drive away* the grievous wolves"; an exhortation which permitted of a mischievous application. The writer of this sketch dare not indulge in comments on the impatience of youth, and there is very little evidence of any kind in the Church records. But what there is is all in John Clayton's favour. The Church was by no means clear of the commercial spirit. The only view of its functions still held by many was that it was a society for managing certain business in connection with the expenses of public worship. That such questions must inevitably arise, and that they should be discussed and answered from a Christian standpoint, is beyond dispute. But it says much for John Clayton that the constant intrusion of the merely financial element, and the failure of those in authority to realise the spiritual mission of the Church, caused him such concern, that he felt compelled to resign his ministry. Possibly he was unprepared for the necessarily slow and difficult work of permeating a society of characteristically business men with the deepest religious spirit. The membership of the Church stood still. Mr. Clayton said that he found his sentiments on many subjects, but especially that of the Lord's Supper, opposed to those of many of the members. He was not himself a man who would be easily carried away with a rush of enthusiasm, and hence he did not carry away others. God was, even then, preparing just such a man to break down the unspirituality of the congregation, and to build up a higher form of Christian society in Kensington; and this man was still at college when John Clayton's resignation was accepted in December, 1804.

PORTRAIT OF REV. DR. JOHN LEIFCHILD

IV

SIXTEEN YEARS OF SPIRITUAL PROGRESS—REV. JOHN LEIFCHILD

IF the congregation at Kensington felt that John Clayton acted with something of the rashness and impatience of youth, there was at least no sign that they so regarded it: for after unsuccessful overtures had been made to the Rev. F. Hamilton, of Brighton, to become successor to Mr. Clayton, they turned to another young man fresh from college, whose name was John Leifchild. After patiently waiting until he had completed the few remaining months of his college course, they welcomed him to the pastorate in June, 1808; and a very remarkable ministry then began. It is impossible to feel surprise at Mr. Leifchild's frank avowal of the defects of the congregation considered as a spiritual society. Any one who has wearily made his way through the minutes in the church-book relating to this period, might be pardoned for concluding that no spiritual body existed at all. The government of the church was in the hands of a small coterie of managers; and the records consist of an uninspiring succession of financial statistics and plans for raising money. To those of us who are more interested in the character of the Church than in the idiosyncrasies of any particular minister, these accounts are not good to read. Mr. Leifchild says, "There was a great prejudice in the town against the Dissenters"; and one can hardly wonder at that when we remember that Dissenters can only justify their existence as Dissenters by the superiority of their spiritual thought and work: and of this at present there is but too little trace in the history that we have received. But in every way—patience, perseverance, tact and courage—John Leifchild was just the man to inaugurate a better era. At this time the church made a resolute and successful endeavour to liquidate the old debt on the buildings: and then, after the manner of high-spirited communities, proceeded to contract a new one. The young minister had almost immediately attained considerable popularity, and a back gallery had to be erected. In a short time side galleries had to be added, to accommodate the people who desired to worship at Hornton Street Chapel. All these alterations involved the congregation in somewhat expensive liabilities, and, in addition, the incidental expenditure had not been met. These were only the necessary penalties of success, and it was quite clear that all would come right in time. But the financial apprehensions of the managers were excited; and they actually formulated proposals for taxing the seat-holders, inserting in their plan, however, a suitable declaration of their devotion to the voluntary principle. The proposals were overthrown by the unwavering resistance of Mr. Leifchild, and the voluntary principle, fairly applied, proved more than adequate to the necessities of the time.

Our Sunday Schools to-day are such a notable feature of Kensington Chapel, that it is interesting to find a record of this kind, dated February 22nd, 1814: "Resolved—In consequence of no other place being found so convenient as the *vault* under the chapel for a Sunday School, that we take the same into consideration." We are sometimes tempted to complain of the discomforts of our present buildings, but those who began the work had to do it obviously under difficulties of which we know little. The managers, however, could not finally consent to bury the Sunday School in the vault,—and hence, by the removal of the staircase, a room was fitted up under the back gallery, and here the Sunday School was very narrowly housed. This important question having been thus disposed of, a more serious problem arose—that of music. There was at this time no organ; but it was natural that one so distinguished in the musical world as Mr. Broadwood should desire the introduction of a suitable instrument. Mr. Broadwood not only desired it; but he was liberal enough to offer to present an organ to the chapel. The conscientious objection to instrumental music in religious buildings is now, for the most part, ancient history. But feeling ran high on the question in the days I am writing of, and one "true-blue Presbyterian," as Dr. Stoughton calls him, would have none of the new-fangled methods, and retired with his family from the scene, entering his protest against the whole proceedings in stout British fashion. Mr. Broadwood gave the organ; and the treasurer had great difficulty, apparently, in paying the organist; and, what with periodical discontinuance of the organ on the score of expense, and criticism of the organist by the congregation, the musical affairs were far from smooth and pleasant for some time to come. Kensington music has never ceased to be a source of anxious solicitude to the Church from that day to this.

Many are the stories of Mr. Leifchild's power of preaching, and it is evident that he prepared his discourses with great care. His method of delivery was somewhat singular, and we should be inclined to regard it as artificial. But it was capable of great effect. The main portion of the discourse was delivered in a quiet, conversational tone, and was occupied in doctrinal, or exegetical, exposition. The audience listened languidly, if not drowsily. But suddenly there was an awakening. The preacher was approaching his application. Standing full back in the pulpit, and mustering all his energy, he proceeded to declaim the final passages of the sermon. In these he drove home the truths he had elicited in exposition with amazing force. The congregation was now listening with breathless interest. This was what they had come to hear; and they were simply at the preacher's mercy for the remainder of his discourse. This old style of preaching has almost entirely, if not altogether, disappeared. But it was a great power in those days, and there were few more absolute masters of the art than John Leifchild. There are still two members connected with Kensington Chapel who were in Mr. Leifchild's Bible Class.

After sixteen years of faithful ministry, Mr. Leifchild accepted a call to Bristol, and left amid genuine expressions of regret. It is interesting to note that, immediately after his departure, the minutes, which have only recorded "Managers' meetings," change to "Managers' and Deacons' meetings." The introduction of the spiritual order of office-bearers is not without significance. Neither is the fact that the next minister was invited, not by the subscribers and trustees, but by the Church. Evidently "the old order changeth, yielding place to new"; and John Leifchild's greatest success was his last—for we can hardly doubt that it was his—when the spiritual order superseded the purely business order, and the power of a body of managers gave way to the authority of a Church of Christ.

PORTRAIT OF REV. DR. ROBERT VAUGHAN

V

PROSPERITY UNDER DR. ROBERT VAUGHAN

In the minutes that describe the events immediately succeeding the resignation of Mr. Leifchild, in August, 1824, there are several references to the institution of a Church Prayer Meeting. Such an anxious period as inevitably follows the loss of a minister is often a valuable discipline to a Church, as tending to throw the members back upon the guidance of the Spirit of God. That the Church at Kensington had realised the need to consult, not only with one another, but with the All-wise, was the best possible augury of prosperity to come. And, verily, God did choose for them. Dr. Robert Vaughan was a very different man in many ways from Mr. Leifchild, but no one could have been more admirably adapted to continue and develop the work that the Church had hitherto been doing. He had all the instincts and tastes of a scholar; and as a brilliant historical writer he exercised a wider ministry, and influenced a larger circle, than if he had simply exercised his gifts as a preacher in the Hornton Street pulpit. So considerable was his fame that he was appointed Professor of Modern History at London University; and, with the generosity which has always characterised the Kensington congregation in such matters, his people spared him gladly much of the labour of visitation, for the sake of the services he was thus able to render to the rising generation of Londoners. Kensington was now assuming the character it has ever since possessed, of a great residential suburb for aristocratic and wealthy London. There was a large circle of able and cultivated men and women to be reached and influenced by the attraction of one, whose personal attainments and powers were sufficiently remarkable to overcome the strong prejudices against Dissenting meeting-places that have always existed in the minds of such. This power Dr. Vaughan possessed and exercised: while at the same time his personal elevation of character, and rare spiritual earnestness, qualified him pre-eminently to be a guide to all who knew him in "the deep things of God." We are consequently quite prepared to find that the little meeting-house in Hornton Street was a centre of light and leading to a large number of men and women who occupied prominent positions in society and in the professions. And yet the last accusation that could be levelled against Dr. Vaughan was that of a "tuft-hunter." He did not *stoop* to conquer, in the sense of descending to any unworthy artifices: he flattered no one; and his reputation as one of the great historians of Nonconformity is sufficient assurance that he never betrayed his trust as a custodian of the sacred interests of religious freedom.

One of the signs of the earnestness of the Church at this time, in seeking to perpetuate the principles for which it stood, was the constant interest manifested in the work of the British Schools, for which Dr. Vaughan repeatedly preached special sermons. The school used to meet in a building at the back of Hornton Street Chapel. No attempt was made to indoctrinate the infant mind with denominational ideas; but, on the other hand, such religious instruction was given as is clearly to be gathered from the study of the Bible, and any child could be educated there without being required to learn by heart the exceedingly questionable teaching of the Church Catechism. For a long period of years these schools remained in very close touch with the Congregational Church, and were only eventually transferred to the management of the School Board when the general scheme of religious education, under the Board, was seen to be thoroughly in harmony with what had prevailed so long in the British Schools.

It is by such simple notices as those concerning the British Schools, the Missionary Society, the Sunday Schools, and other institutions, that we can form our idea of the many interests that were beginning to take possession of the hearts of the people. The records during Dr. Vaughan's ministry are singularly imperfect, and it is only quite incidentally that we get some impression of the steadily increasing prosperity of the cause. For eighteen years Dr. Vaughan continued his ministry, and there is not a single evidence of a moment's break in the harmony of the Church. When, in 1843, Dr. Vaughan was honoured with an invitation to become Principal of the Lancashire Independent College, the letters of himself and of the Church were such as became those who had lived and worked so long together in the most honourable spirit of Christian fellowship. The letter of the Church is exceedingly touching in its anxiety to express to the full its ardent and affectionate attachment to Dr. Vaughan, and yet to do nothing to add to the necessary pain and anxiety of his decision. Dr. Vaughan felt that the call to Lancashire was of God, and he placed his resignation in the hands of the Church. But even then, his interest in their welfare was unabated; and he knew the perils of a time of unsettlement. There was one well known to him, and to whom he was related by many affinities of thought and sympathy, who was labouring at that time in a sphere of less influence at Windsor; and, before he left Kensington, he approached Dr. John Stoughton, and obtained from him the promise that he would consent to preach before the Kensington congregation. Two months afterwards Dr. Stoughton accepted a unanimous invitation from the Church, and commenced his ministry. Before closing this chapter, one word must be added. There are many sacred memories connected with Hornton Street Chapel, and those who used to worship there; but none more sacred to all who honour those in whom pure genius stands united to simple faith and devout spirituality, than those associated with the name of Robert Alfred Vaughan. He was the beloved son of Dr. Vaughan, and the highest hopes were cherished for him by a large circle of religious and literary men. He entered the Congregational ministry, and gave to the world a work of the greatest promise, entitled "Hours with the Mystics." His own beautiful spirit breathed through every page. But his work was too arduous, and he died in early manhood. It has been said that if he had avoided the fatigue of constant pastoral duty, he might have lived on to do brilliant intellectual work. It may be so. But perhaps he chose the better part, and did the greater work, as will one day be known. At any rate, he has left us his own answer, in what has been called his "Psalm of Life."

> "And thou canst not in life's city
> Rule thy course as in a cell:
> There are others, all thy brothers,
> Who have work to do as well.
>
> "Some events that mar thy purpose
> May light *them* upon their way;
> Our sun—shining, in declining—
> Gives earth's other side the day.
>
> "Every star is drawn and draweth
> 'Mid the orbits of its peers;
> And the blending thus unending
> Makes the music of the spheres."

Of Robert Alfred Vaughan we still love to conjecture what he *is*, or, as some prefer to put it, what he would have been if he had lived. He was the Arthur Hallam of Nonconformity.

PORTRAIT OF REV. DR. JOHN STOUGHTON

VI

ENLARGING OUR BORDERS—REV. DR. STOUGHTON'S MINISTRY.

THE succession of Dr. Stoughton to the ministry of the Church brings us exactly to the middle of our century of history. In October, 1843, the recognition service was held. Dr. Stoughton, in his letter accepting the invitation, had feelingly referred to the difficulty of following Dr. Vaughan, "one whose eminence in the Christian world might well provoke, in connection with myself, humiliating comparisons." But, indeed, the Church had been guided to one of the very few men who might fittingly continue the work of Dr. Vaughan. As a historian of those periods of English history in which Nonconformists are especially interested, Dr. Stoughton stands unsurpassed among Englishmen; and such is the fairness and moderation of his writings that Church of England lecturers have repeatedly made appeal to them as models of impartial and accurate statement. Indeed, Dr. Stoughton's literary industry has been immense. The Religious Tract Society has largely benefited by admirably written accounts of the great Reformers and religious heroes of Christendom, while Dr. Stoughton's editorship of the *Evangelical Magazine* was conspicuously successful in making that organ a power among the Churches. But it was in no partial or half-hearted way that he threw himself into his ministerial work at Kensington. Our readers must turn to his own inimitable narrative in "Congregationalism in the Court Suburb" for the delightful reminiscences he gives of his own ministry, and the people associated with it. Our concern is with the growth of the Church life; and to this end we must pursue our examination of the records, which are henceforth admirably kept.

That Dr. Stoughton immediately acquired the full confidence and loyal support of the Church officers and members is evident from a very remarkable fact. For many years past the Church had been, in all essential procedure, a Congregational Church; but, although it was so in fact, it was not so actually in form. The members had apparently not been led to see the importance of constituting themselves according to the New Testament practice. We all know that it is not easy to carry out important changes without arousing considerable criticism, and, not unusually, opposition. And for the truer fashioning of the Church upon more Apostolic lines there was needed a strong and wise leadership. This leadership was supplied by the new minister, and the delicate work of reorganisation was most successfully and harmoniously carried through. The existing "managers" became deacons, and new deacons were appointed; and the Church assumed the form which it has ever since maintained. It was of excellent augury for the success of his ministry that Dr. Stoughton perceived so early that the recognition of the spiritual order of the Church in form, as well as in fact, was a vital principle. However much of the subsequent development of our Church we may attribute to Dr. Stoughton's able and devoted ministry, we are bound to attribute even more to this bold and timely assertion of the true idea of the Church.

HORBURY CHAPEL, NOTTING HILL

The time soon came when the Hornton Street Chapel proved too small for the number of hearers. Kensington was, even now, rapidly developing, and every month added to the congregations that assembled to worship in what was never a large building. What enlargement could easily be made was carried out in 1845, but it afforded only temporary relief. There had evidently come to the Church one of those testing times of faith and sacrifice which prove the genuineness of the spirit and the life. The district of Notting Hill was becoming an influential and populous one, and the conviction was laying hold of the minds and hearts of many, that it was a clear duty to Christ that a certain number of the members should consent to break with the old associations of Hornton Street, and form a new Church in the district just mentioned. Such a proposal, of course, meant even more than the severance of very sacred ties that bound them to the old society, and to their loved minister. It meant a generous offering of their money for the new building. But to all these demands the Church was equal. At a meeting held in the vestry at Hornton Street, £1700 was at once subscribed, and, in a very tender and beautiful document, that betrays in every line the sorrow that they felt at thus going forth from a place and a community so dear to them, thirty-seven members ask to be commissioned by the Hornton Street Church to form a new society at Horbury, Notting Hill. An exodus of this kind, where the spirit is entirely of love and faith, is a memorable and impressive event. Something like one hundred seat-holders left Hornton Street for Horbury; but the two congregations remained one in heart, as they were one in tradition. Under the long and able ministry of the Rev. William Roberts, the Horbury Church has been a great power for good in that neighbourhood. We reproduce a photograph of the chapel, which stands on an admirable site, and presents a very good appearance.

On purely economical principles the mother Church should now be seriously weakened by the voluntary surrender of so many members, and so much earnest Christian capacity. But the great law of the economy of the Kingdom of Heaven is that we live by sacrifice. And it was so now. The Church at Hornton Street flourished as never before. The income was not impaired: the sittings refilled; the organisations abounded with life. In influence, reputation, and spiritual power, the Church grew day by day. Not five years afterwards, the old problem of enlarging the accommodation presented itself once more for solution. The time was hardly ripe, nor was any special neighbourhood obvious, for planting a new settlement. Consequently the alternative solution remained. There must be a new and larger edifice built. The spirit of the people, so far from being daunted by the prospect of a large expenditure, and all the infinite cares of chapel building, rose to meet the opportunity. The site at Allen Street was secured, and in June, 1854, Dr. Stoughton laid the first stone of Kensington Chapel. In May, 1855, the building was opened, and in January, 1860, it was paid for, the total cost of land and building being £8748 9s. 6d. The plain and severe character of the interior probably represented, even then, the average Nonconformist taste in regard to chapel architecture. Æsthetically considered, it is no doubt indefensible. The windows are undeniably ugly; the pulpit—designed as a firm remonstrance against locomotion on the part of its occupant—is painfully stiff and square; and the general aspect of the building is somewhat dull and prosaic. But, as a suitable and convenient place for Nonconformist worship, there is very much to be said for this form of building. Every one can see the preacher, and he can see every one. The acoustic properties are perfect.

Nothing interferes with the enjoyment of speaking and hearing: no handsome but troublesome pillars interrupt the sight; and, let us add, when it is well filled, many of its most obvious defects entirely disappear.

There is no need to trace in anything like detail the steady progress of the Church in its new habitation. In 1856 the Lecture Hall was built, and has been an indispensable adjunct to the Church buildings since that time. In 1868 the Church took into consideration the need for larger buildings to contain the British Schools, and shortly afterwards the friends of the Schools began the building that now stands next to Kensington Chapel, and is the meeting-place of our Sunday Schools. Thus the years were full of work and growth in many directions, and the utmost harmony prevailed among the members, while the relationship of pastor and people grew closer and more affectionate as the time rolled by. In course of time the Church provided an assistant minister to relieve Dr. Stoughton of some part of the labour. The arrangement worked harmoniously and fairly successfully. But Dr. Stoughton had come to feel that this was not a permanent settlement of the question that was arising, how best to provide for the pastoral supervision of the people, as well as for the superintendence of the numerous important organisations connected with the Church. Through thirty years of faithful ministerial labour, assisted by the harmonious co-operation of a devoted people, Dr. Stoughton had led the Church forward, step by step, into a position of exceptional strength and influence. It was not unnatural that, having borne the burden and heat of the day so faithfully and so long, he should desire to be released from the full responsibilities of the pastorate. But it was two years later before his deeply attached people could consent to the severance of a tie that had become so sacred. The retirement of Dr. Stoughton from the pastorate of the Church evoked demonstrations of respect and affection that we do not hesitate to term unique. At the public meeting in the chapel, on April 8th, 1875, to say farewell, there was a most remarkable assemblage of honoured men. Mr. Samuel Morley occupied the chair, and Sir Thomas Chambers, Mr. Henry Richard, Sir Charles Reed, Dean Stanley, Canon Fremantle, Dr. Morley Punshon, Dr. Angus, Dr. Henry Allon, and the Rev. Baldwin Brown were among those who took part in the meeting. An address, expressive of admiration and regard for Dr. Stoughton, and gratitude for his devoted ministry, was presented to him, accompanied by a purse containing £3000. Thus closed a most memorable ministry. But it is one of the special joys of our centenary services that Dr. Stoughton should still be able to come among us, to celebrate the fiftieth year of his association with Kensington. He retired full of honours. His great qualities, alike of literary ability and personal character, won for him the unique distinction of being elected by those most eminent in the various branches of our national life—Politics, Art, Science, and Literature—to membership of the Athenæum Club. We believe that he alone of all Nonconformist ministers has been welcomed to this honour. But we are certainly right in saying that, even more than such a mark of recognition by men distinguished in so many walks of life, he has valued the simple love and loyalty of that Christian Church to which he gave himself with such unqualified devotion, and which owes so much of its present character and influence to the spiritual leadership of Dr. Stoughton.

PORTRAIT OF REV. DR. ALEXANDER RALEIGH

VII

A GRACIOUS MINISTRY—DR. ALEXANDER RALEIGH

A DISTINGUISHED living preacher once said to his congregation that his work would only be done when he had taught them to do without him. It is a true test of the soundness of a minister's work when the congregation does not break up, nor even suffer loss at his withdrawal, but, in the spirit of faith and prayer and counsel, addresses itself to the delicate work of seeking a successor. A congregation, that for thirty-two years had enjoyed the ministry of so able a man as Dr. Stoughton, might have almost been forgiven, had it manifested some indecision when his guidance was withdrawn. But a true Independent Church is trained to habits of self-government; and at the critical periods of its history these habits are its protection and salvation. After unavailing efforts had been made to induce the Rev. G. S. Barrett, B.A., of Norwich, to accept the pastorate, the thought of the Church was directed to one whose name will ever be fragrant in the memory of the Church of Christ, Dr. Alexander Raleigh. At this time Dr. Raleigh was exercising his ministry in connection with two associated churches in Highbury; and only the strain of this exceptional work upon one of his advancing years could justify him in listening to any proposals that he should move westward. The work at Highbury was in the highest degree fruitful: but it was evident that Dr. Raleigh's health was on the verge of breaking down; and when the cordial and unanimous call of the Kensington Church reached him he gave it earnest and anxious consideration, and finally determined to accept it.

In this way there was consummated a union of which those who were privileged to share in it speak to this day in the most tender and grateful terms. One feels that the very chapel has been hallowed and consecrated by the closing years of a beautiful ministry—years which brought with them all the radiant hues and tints of autumn. The story of these years, as, indeed, of the whole life of Alexander Raleigh, has been so inimitably written by his wife, that it has become a classic among Nonconformist biographies; and there are few libraries among us on the shelves of which there are not to be found "Quiet Resting-places," "The Little Sanctuary," "The Book of Esther," or some other volume of those exquisitely finished and spiritual sermons which will embody the spirit of Alexander Raleigh for all future generations. Dr. Raleigh, especially at this period of his life, had an indefinable grace of spiritual repose and inward peace, which communicated itself to those who came under his influence. Not that he was a Quietist. He was an ardent politician, and never ceased to take a profound and practical interest in questions of national importance. He was an impassioned preacher of righteousness; and a robust and uncompromising Nonconformist. But controversy did not disturb his deep inward peace of spirit; and while it is true that, like the great Independent of earlier days,

> "His heart
> The lowliest duties on herself did lay";

it could also be said of him,

> "Thy soul was like a star and dwelt apart."

But it would be impossible to speak of Dr. Raleigh's work at Kensington without speaking of Mrs. Raleigh's work also. It is still a red-letter day in the experience of many at Kensington Chapel when Mrs. Raleigh revisits those in whose hearts she has so large a place, and to many of whom she made real the most sacred beliefs of Christianity. Mrs. Raleigh gathered a large Bible Class, which still continues to assemble in the Deacons' Vestry on Sunday afternoons, and comprises not only elder girls and young women, but those who would not be offended if they were called elderly. The character of her influence over this class, and over all in the congregation who knew her—and who did not?—needs to be actually known to be adequately appreciated.

The congregations, under Dr. Raleigh's inspiring ministry, filled the large chapel in every part. And, with this growth in the congregation, it must have been very encouraging, to all who were interested, to mark the growth in the Church. At one time forty-three members are recorded as having joined the Church, at another time thirty, at another twenty-five, and so on. Many who were of Scotch extraction found their patriotism too strong even for denominational preferences, and came great distances to hear "Raleigh" at Kensington. Brief as his ministry was—too brief, we say, with our imperfect conceptions—it was yet long enough to leave an indelible impression on numbers of his hearers, who will bear the marks of his fashioning to all eternity. His successors in the ministry here alone know, perhaps, how deep and abiding was the spiritual work done in those five years.

That, in the enjoyment of these rare spiritual privileges, the Church did not become self-centred, is manifest, not only in the steady interest in missionary and philanthropic work, but in the initiation of a movement, which was not realised until later, for planting a new church at West Kensington. With characteristic generosity Dr. Raleigh welcomed the proposal, but it was not given to him to do more than "greet the promise afar." The shadow was even now beginning to fall upon him; yet those who had been most apprehensive of a serious breakdown in his health learned with something of stupefaction the doctors' verdict that recovery was impossible. There is a deeply pathetic suggestiveness associated with the fact that the last sermon he preached was from the text, "And Enoch walked with God: and he was not, for God took him." Possibly some premonition of the end had come to him; possibly a Higher than he had put the words into his heart for his final address to his beloved people. For the touching story of his last days, we shall still turn to the beautiful narrative of Mrs. Raleigh. It is not too much to say that not only all Congregationalists everywhere kept sympathetic watch, as it were, around the sick-bed; but the larger Church of Christ listened anxiously for tidings of the progress of the invalid. And progress it was, but progress heavenward. Shortly after noon on Monday, April 19th, 1880, he passed away; and, for the first time in its history, Death had sealed the ministry of a pastor of the Kensington Church while he was still in its service. There is a holy discipline for a Church in such a deep common sorrow, such as not the most eloquent preaching can convey. The "still" voice speaks louder even than the strong full voice of life. It is good sometimes for the soul of a people to be humbled by a great grief. At no past time had an experience so searching as this come to the Church at Kensington. Its pastors had left it for other work and other spheres. But this one had died among them; in the very ripeness of his powers he had passed away. All the demonstrations of their sorrow were but a weak expression of what they felt. And yet there was a meaning in the visitation; and one cannot doubt that out of their minister's cheerful serenity, and calm and tranquil "exodus," God wrought for them a quickening of faith. For of Alexander Raleigh it might well be said that the "manner of his passing" was an "evidence of the things unseen."

PORTRAIT OF REV. COLMER B. SYMES

VIII

PLANTING A NEW CHURCH—MR. C. B. SYMES' MINISTRY

"God buries His workers, but carries on His work." It is this faith that leads a Church, even under the shock of a bereavement as severe as this one had been, to turn with unabated determination to the prosecution of the work. The more nearly a Church of Christ attains the standard of the Master, the less it depends on any mere human instrumentality for its success. It is not the person of the preacher, but the Person of the Christ and the love of His work, that forms the sacred tie between the members. This it is that prevents the work of God from suffering, and gives permanence to His cause. It was truly with a sad heart that the Church assembled at this time to consult about a successor to Dr. Raleigh; but the claims of "the work" were paramount, and there was a plain but difficult duty before them. Our critics are not slow to remind us that the gravest defect of the Congregational system lies in the fact that, during the period when a church is without a minister, a system of competition among rival candidates is pursued, which is humiliating to the self-respect of those who preach, and calculated to provoke division and contention among those who sit in judgment. This evil is, we believe, being resolutely redressed in most of our Churches to-day, and the Kensington Church has never suffered from it at any period of its history. A trusted committee made careful inquiries with a view to discovering some minister who seemed to be adapted, alike in character and abilities, to the special wants of this neighbourhood. Opportunity was then sought of introducing him to the pulpit, and if he manifestly commended himself to the whole Church—and not a mere majority of the Church—he was invited to become the minister. This admirable plan has averted anything like the evils sometimes associated with a change of pastorate. In the instance before us the committee's attention was directed to the eminently successful ministry of the Rev. Colmer B. Symes, B.A., of Exeter. In that corner of England Mr. Symes had most worthily maintained for several years the office of the Christian ministry, and had exercised a great power for good. All who knew him esteemed him for the loftiness of his Christian character, as well as for his ministerial gifts. As a man of culture and wide reading, he seemed to be conspicuously suited to the special needs of a locality, where the problems of modern thought occupied the minds of a large proportion of the population. Mr. Symes preached at Kensington, with no intention whatever of being a "candidate": but as there was an immediate response to his message, a unanimous invitation was sent to him to become the pastor of the Church, and in January, 1881, Mr. Symes was recognised as the minister.

The Church records contain many testimonies to the power of the ministry thus begun. The number of Church members steadily grew. The monthly Church meetings were times of continual rejoicing over accessions to the ranks of those who had solemnly taken the sacred pledge of loyalty to Christ. So high was the spirit of the Church, that, in the second year of Mr. Symes' ministry, it was decided vigorously to pursue the movement, initiated in Dr. Raleigh's pastorate, of building a new Congregational church at West Kensington. Nothing was more characteristic of the new minister than the cordiality with which he furthered a scheme that must inevitably diminish, at any rate for a time, his own Church and congregation. Thinking, rather, of the necessities of the rapidly growing neighbourhood of West Kensington, Mr. Symes and his Church threw themselves nobly into the enterprise. At a meeting held in the Vestry Hall, Kensington, it was announced that no less a sum than £12,084 had been promised, and the whole cost of over £15,000 was raised at the opening of the church.

Not thirty years had passed since the opening of Allen Street Chapel, but the new church at West Kensington would seem to indicate a remarkable change in taste and idea as regards the character of ecclesiastical buildings. It is a conspicuously handsome building, with a massive central tower, a chancel, and a general elegance of structure not unworthy to rank among the very best of modern Nonconformist Church edifices. We are all of us familiar with the natural law which leads parents to be far more lavish in expenditure for their children than for themselves. We are consequently not surprised to find that the Church at Allen Street spent twice as much on a building for this child of its own training as it did on the building in which the mother Church still worships. At a special Church meeting, that strikingly recalls the moving and interesting gathering when the first branch Church removed from Kensington to Notting Hill, nearly thirty members took a farewell of Allen Street, and went to the new and difficult work of building up a strong church in West Kensington; and with them went naturally a considerable number of seat-holders, supported in their action by the generous encouragement of the Allen Street minister. Thus the second colony was planted from the mother Church. She had given lavishly of her own life and treasure for the enrichment of others; and by the eternal law of the Cross she reaped her reward in the fuller and deeper life bestowed upon those who remained. There only remains to add that, after years of hard and discouraging labour, the new Church appears to be slowly and steadily rooting itself, and to be destined to become a spiritual power in the locality.

WEST KENSINGTON CONGREGATIONAL CHURCH

Uneventful years followed. Those who best know the character of modern Kensington are best able to appreciate the difficulty there is of gathering a strong evening congregation. With his previous successful experience at Exeter so fresh in his memory, it is no wonder that Mr. Symes felt, even more acutely than many do who are called to minister in the West of London, this grave discouragement to the preacher. Many of his expedients to meet the difficulty were for a time successful. Largely-attended evangelistic services were periodically held; but the permanent evening congregation did not grow. Still more serious a problem to one of Mr. Symes' intensely earnest temperament was the decline in the number of those who were led to public acknowledgment of a change of life. He could not reconcile his own conception of what justifies a ministry in any place with the absence of this note of success; and hence, in a characteristically beautiful letter to the Church in March, 1887, he placed his resignation in their hands. The remarkable meeting at which the congregation presented to Mr. Symes a large portrait in oils of himself, and an illuminated address, was the occasion of a demonstration of the affection and regard in which he was universally held. There have been resignations of ministers who have been determined in their action by a variety of considerations that have led them to give the preference to one sphere of labour over another. But surely the highest of all considerations is contained in so deep a sense of the spiritual mission of the minister, and in so lofty an ideal of his work, that even a qualified response to the public and private ministrations suggests that a continuance of the ministry may cause the interests of the Kingdom to suffer. The Kensington Church had had many lessons before this time, from those who had made great and cheerful sacrifices for its interests; but such a lesson was never taught it with more of real Christian dignity and chivalry than when Mr. Symes laid down the office of minister; thus ending a six years' pastorate for which very many of the congregation to-day continue to thank God.

PORTRAIT OF REV. EDWARD WHITE

IX

A NOTABLE INTERVAL—REV. EDWARD WHITE

At the time of Mr. Symes' resignation, the present minister of the church was a freshman at College, and a good deal more occupied with studies and athletics than with any question of settling in the ministry. It was not really a surprising thing to those who knew the traditions of Kensington Chapel, that a Church that had chosen John Clayton when he was twenty-one, and that had waited for Mr. Leifchild until he had completed his college course, should elect to wait nearly two years for its present minister. The course was an unusual one, but it had one conspicuous advantage. It enabled the Church to enjoy for eighteen months the ministry of the Rev. Edward White. It is unnecessary to explain to any one who knows any thing of Congregationalism, or the history of theological thought during the last half century, who Mr. Edward White is. There had been a time when he was suspected and misunderstood, for having interpreted the teaching of Scripture on one point in a sense different from the majority of his brethren. But we live in happier days, when our joy is to dwell rather on our substantial unity than on points of different interpretation. Mr. White has won the recognition of the whole Catholic Church as a stalwart standard-bearer in the "good fight of faith"; and great was the satisfaction at Kensington, when one who was just retiring from an arduous and remarkable ministry at Kentish Town was willing to give himself to the superintendence of the work at Kensington, until the minister-elect had completed his college training.

The result of this arrangement was exceedingly happy. We believe Mr. White was rewarded by the multitude of new friends that he thus made; and the congregation was abundantly rewarded, not only by the steady advance in interest that was made during the time of Mr. White's ministry, but by the securing for itself of the sympathy and affection of such a friend as Mr. White has been. The young men remember to-day with the keenest relish the good times they had in Mr. White's Bible Class; and, indeed, he has only to appear among us to evoke the loudest demonstrations of welcome. But in nothing did his loving and genial spirit appear more characteristically than in his relations with the one who was appointed to succeed him in the ministry at Kensington. The writer of this book records here the lasting debt of gratitude he is under to Mr. White for tender and helpful counsel and loving encouragement, such as he can never cease to remember with filial reverence and thankfulness.

The minister of a Church such as ours is always interested in discovering the "deposit" of well-remembered sayings and stories of the various ministers and prominent laymen that have been associated with the place. There grows up in this way a kind of Rabbinical tradition; and you can often estimate the force of character in a minister by the way in which people treasure up the memories of what he said and did. Mr. White added materially to the oral tradition of Kensington. His racy sayings, his epigrams, his reminiscences, are constantly recalled and repeated. And his successor has formed a very vivid conception of that genial and delightful ministry by which Mr. White attached to himself so warmly the hearts of this congregation.

But one most significant new departure must be remembered. Many are the strangers who visit us to-day who are greatly impressed with the successful blending in our service of general audible prayer, with the more individual prayer by the minister. They share with us the feeling, that to encourage an outward and audible expression of our worship is to cultivate the worshipful attitude of heart and soul. Nonconformists have too long thrown the whole burden of the service on the preacher, and not sufficiently elicited from the congregation the full expression of their feelings in prayer and praise. The new warmth that has come to our services at Allen Street, and the increased heartiness of them, is very largely due to the introduction of certain simple and comprehensive forms of worship and prayer, in which we can all unite with heart and soul. This most admirable system was initiated by Mr. White, who expressed himself as being quite willing to bear the burden of any temporary unpopularity of the change. The unpopularity was certainly never great, and has to-day given way to a very strong and general satisfaction.

Resolutions are apt to read coldly,—indeed, they are apt not to be read at all,—but when, at a large meeting of the Church and congregation to say farewell to Mr. White, on the completion of his eighteen months' ministry, the people unanimously and enthusiastically declared that "he had been honoured to become the channel of blessings which this Church would ever acknowledge and keep in memory," every word was as hearty as it was true. On October 17th, 1889, Mr. White presided at his successor's ordination, and said to the assembled people: "In delivering up this sacred office, I shall humbly join my prayers with yours for God's best blessing to rest on my dear successor, and on yourselves, whom he will love the more the longer he lives among you, and the more self-denyingly he serves you." To which that successor may be allowed to write his own emphatic declaration that it has been true.

PORTRAIT OF REV. C. SILVESTER HORNE

X

"TO BE CONTINUED"—THE PRESENT PASTORATE
(MR. HORNE)[2]

THE retirement of a pastor so universally beloved as Mr. Symes left the Church in a position of some perplexity, from which it was to be rescued less by its own wisdom than by the manifest leading of Providence. For more than sixty years the congregation had welcomed to its pastorate ministers already enjoying reputations acquired in other Churches; and in the eyes of many this practice had acquired the authority of a traditionary rule. And it seems almost certain that, if any of the established ministers whom the Church would have been glad to call would have accepted what was recognised as an onerous charge, the traditions of 1825–80 would have been honoured by continued observance. But it was otherwise ordained. While as yet no one seems to have remembered how Dr. Leifchild came to Hornton Street fresh from his tutor, Mr. Charles Silvester Horne, a student only half through his theological course at Mansfield College, Oxford, came to Kensington as an ordinary pulpit supply, and preached with so much acceptance that request was made,—but without any ulterior view,—that he might be sent again. He had preached only a very few times, however, when it became evident that he was not only making a strong impression on the existing congregation, but attracting new hearers. It was noticed that, while the freshness and simplicity of his preaching, aided by a genial personality, drew simple natures, and especially the young, around him, the confidence of the elders was gained by the unexpected depth and maturity of his sermons; and then it was that the suppressed thought of many at length found simultaneous utterance, and the question was asked whether this was not the kind of minister most suited to the wants of the Kensington congregation.

Inquiries were made, and then it was ascertained that Mr. Horne had still eighteen months of his course at Mansfield to complete, and that of these Dr. Fairbairn would not abate even a week. By this time, however, the Church had made up its mind, and unanimously offered to pledge itself to call Mr. Horne in due form at the end of a year and a half, if he, in his turn, would engage to come to Kensington at that date, and also visit the congregation in the meantime as often as he could. This arrangement was made, together with a further and supplementary one with the Rev. Edward White, who had just left Kentish Town, and who kindly undertook the pastoral oversight of the Church till the autumn of 1889. In this way, as was pleasantly observed at the time, Kensington at once secured the services of

[2] By a Member of the Congregation.

"the youngest old man and the oldest young man in the Congregational body." Mr. White more than fulfilled the expectations of the congregation, and in the brief period of his service established himself permanently in the affections of the congregation, while he prepared the way for the coming of his young successor.

Mr. Horne was ordained at Kensington in October 1889, the venerable Dr. Stoughton, Dr. Fairbairn, and Dr. Dale, with the Revs. E. White, R. F. Horton, and W. Roberts, taking part in the services. This is not the time to speak at large of a pastorate so recently begun, but it is not too soon to say that the hopes on which the Kensington Church acted five years ago have been justified by experience. Congregations were never larger; the young are being gathered and organised in guilds as well for instruction and work as for social purposes; the young members of the Church meet regularly for spiritual edification. The London Missionary Society and other agencies external to the congregation are supported with the old constancy and liberality, and the Church itself is as united as ever in purpose and heart.

KENSINGTON CHAPEL (INTERIOR)

XI

EPILOGUE

A MINISTER may surely be excused for writing "once more, in conclusion," after the "lastly" of Chapter IX. He is, however, quite prepared to see the reader grow indifferent or uneasy, under the impression that the epilogue has been dragged in with the ulterior intention of pointing a moral. The story has been told; what need can there be to prolong it? But so hardened has the writer become that he unmercifully proceeds to have his own way—a bad habit, into which a too-indulgent congregation has injudiciously trained him. The perusal of our simple records is calculated to confirm the faith of us all in the possibilities of a Church of Jesus Christ. Dr. Stoughton likes to say that the Church here was never asked for money when it did not meet the request; and, perhaps, that is the least of all its gifts. Its chronicler lays down the pen with the thankful conviction that it has ever given a place in its heart and in its practical sympathy to any really worthy and beneficent object. Its controversies have been conducted in honourable Christian fashion, and where its convictions have been deep its efforts have been unremitting. Perhaps the truest test of a Church is in the men and women it makes and influences. Kensington Chapel has been associated with many eminent and brilliant names. Lawyers such as Mr. Justice Talfourd, statesmen such as Mr. Henry Richard, physicians such as Sir Risdon Bennett, authors such as Dr. Samuel Smiles and Robert Alfred Vaughan, as well as Royal Academicians and influential writers for the public press, have united here in common worship. And lest we should be overwhelmed, and unduly sobered, by so great a weight of dignity, was there not once an editor of *Punch* as a member of the congregation? Who will say of us that our Puritan manners are irreconcilable with a love of humour!

"Diversity of ministrations but the same spirit" seems to have been the law of Apostolical succession in this Church. The ministers have been very unlike one another; but there has been a great substance of truth which they have preached, and an unbroken unity of purpose and aim. Those who think a Church needs thirty-nine articles to ensure the unity of the spirit will please make a note of this.

The Church has been distinguished for its readiness of adjustment to new opportunities and occasions. The development of modern London has drawn Kensington from its position of a secluded proximity to the City, into actual organic union with it. All the problems of London to-day are ours. We are no longer outside of it. Our life is Metropolitan. The change has been faced by the Church with a frank recognition and a cheerful courage. It has acknowledged practically the claims of poorer London on its liberality and sympathy; and it is resolutely addressing itself to discover its own distinctive mission to the poverty and misery of other neighbourhoods.

It was clearly not for nothing that the idea of the Church emerged slowly but surely out of the looser conceptions of association for the purpose of managing the business affairs connected with a place of worship. God's hand was in it all, as we can so clearly see to-day; and in process of the years the great ideal of a Christian Brotherhood—an ideal which is not new, but old—has laid hold of the thought and imagination of the people. Dr. Edwin Hatch, the most original ecclesiastical historian of this generation, said in memorable words, "the unaccomplished mission of the Christian Church is to reconstruct society on the basis of brotherhood." Towards that reconstruction every Christian community that tries to realise its brotherhood in Christ contributes something.

At the beginning of the century whose record we have reviewed, Missionary Societies were just beginning, Sunday Schools were in their infancy, and the great catalogue of benevolent and philanthropic societies that stand on the Church's list was all unknown. Thus the work of one hundred years makes us exceedingly hopeful. Our experience is all in our favour. And after having lived and grown through a century of time, it is possible for us, as a Church, to approximate to that ideal where there are blended the ripeness and maturity of autumn with the freshness and buoyancy of spring.

Lector House believes that a society develops through a two-fold approach of continuous learning and adaptation, which is derived from the study of classic literary works spread across the historic timeline of literature records. Therefore, we aim at reviving, repairing and redeveloping all those inaccessible or damaged but historically as well as culturally important literature across subjects so that the future generations may have an opportunity to study and learn from past works to embark upon a journey of creating a better future.

This book is a result of an effort made by Lector House towards making a contribution to the preservation and repair of original ancient works which might hold historical significance to the approach of continuous learning across subjects.

HAPPY READING & LEARNING!

LECTOR HOUSE LLP
E-MAIL: lectorpublishing@gmail.com